discovermore

Learning Social Studies Skills

Exploring Primary Sources

Marie Harts

Britannica Educational Publishing

IN ASSOCIATION WITH

THE ROSEN PUBLISHING GROUP

Published in 2025 by The Rosen Publishing Group, Inc.
2544 Clinton Street, Buffalo, NY 14224

Editor: Shannon Harts
Book Design: Michael Flynn

Photo Credits: Cover Sean Locke Photography/Shutterstock.com; (series background) Dai Yim/Shutterstock.com; pp. 4, 15, 16 courtesy of the Library of Congress; p. 5 Kaspars Grinvalds/Shutterstock.com; p. 6 Diego Grandi/Shutterstock.com; p. 7 https://commons.wikimedia.org/wiki/File:Broadside_of_John_Brown%27s_last_speech.jpg; p. 8 lev radin/Shutterstock.com; p. 9 https://commons.wikimedia.org/wiki/File:Oral_history_baltimore.jpg; p. 11 (top) https://commons.wikimedia.org/wiki/File:Aramaic_Papyrus_with_Story_of_Ahiqar.jpg; p. 11 (bottom) mark reinstein/Shutterstock.com; p. 12 https://commons.wikimedia.org/wiki/File:Former_Soviet_Pilot_Viktor_Belenko%E2%80%99s_Military_Identity_Document.jpg; p. 13 Takashi Images/Shutterstock.com; pp. 14, 22 Everett Collection/Shutterstock.com; p. 17 Alex from the Rock/Shutterstock.com; p. 18 Vadim_N/Shutterstock.com; p. 19 Yogi Nugroho/Shutterstock.com; p. 21 (top) DimaBerlin/Shutterstock.com; p. 21 (bottom) Artush/Shutterstock.com; p. 23 vchal/Shutterstock.com; p. 24 Dan Shachar/Shutterstock.com; p. 25 https://commons.wikimedia.org/wiki/File:Destruction_of_Palmyra_by_Islamic_State_(28305884430).jpg; p. 27 (top) AhBoon.Net/Shutterstock.com; p. 27 (bottom) https://commons.wikimedia.org/wiki/File:Portrait_of_Paquius_Proculo_restored.jpg; p. 28 https://commons.wikimedia.org/wiki/File:Allard_Pierson_Museum_Mother_and_child_lekyth_7788.jpg; p. 29 p. 28 Barbara Kalbfleisch/Shutterstock.com.

Library of Congress Cataloging-in-Publication Data

Names: Harts, Marie, author.
Title: Exploring primary sources / Marie Harts.
Description: [Buffalo] : Britannica Educational Publishing, 2025. | Series: Discover more! learning social studies skills | Includes index.
Identifiers: LCCN 2023051596 (print) | LCCN 2023051597 (ebook) | ISBN 9781641901444 (library binding) | ISBN 9781641901437 (paperback) | ISBN 9781641901451 (ebook)
Subjects: LCSH: History--Research--Juvenile literature. | History--Sources.
Classification: LCC D16 .H347 2025 (print) | LCC D16 (ebook) | DDC 907.2--dc23/eng/20231102
LC record available at https://lccn.loc.gov/2023051596
LC ebook record available at https://lccn.loc.gov/2023051597

Manufactured in the United States of America

Some of the images in this book illustrate individuals who are models. The depictions do not imply actual situations or events.

CPSIA Compliance Information: Batch #CSBRIT25. For further information contact Rosen Publishing at 1-800-237-9932.

Contents

Primary Sources Defined

First-hand accounts of history from someone who experienced an event at the time of the event are called primary sources. Some primary sources supply facts about a subject. Other primary sources express, or voice, the views of people who experienced events.

A secondary source does not give original information. It interprets or summarizes information from primary sources. Textbooks, biographies, encyclopedias, and dictionaries are normally secondary sources.

Bob Adelman took this picture of Dr. Martin Luther King Jr. delivering his famous "I Have a Dream" speech. It is considered a primary source.

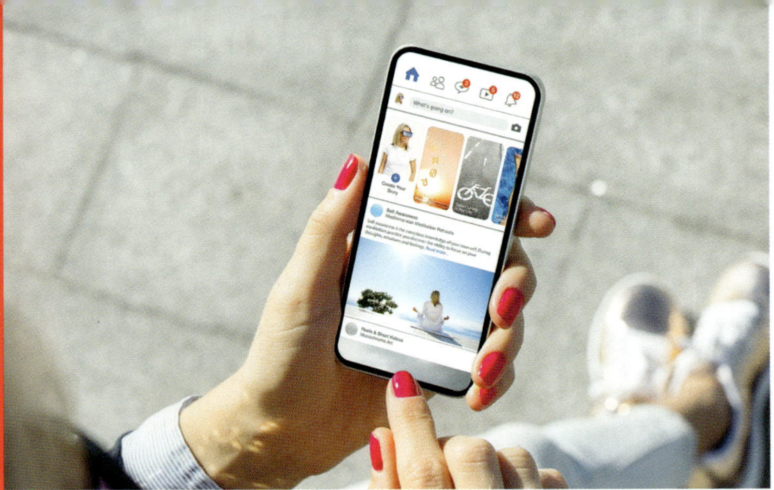

Social media posts, such as those you might have seen on Facebook and Instagram, can be considered primary sources because they are often created about events as the events are happening.

A book about the American Revolution that was written in the 2000s is a secondary source. A journal that a soldier kept during the American Revolution is a primary source.

Sometimes, the way a source is used determines if it counts as primary or secondary. For example, an article about Dr. Martin Luther King Jr.'s "I Have a Dream" speech written during the 1980s wouldn't be considered a primary source about the speech because it was written around 20 years after this speech was given in 1963. However, it could be considered a primary source regarding how people during the 1980s viewed this speech.

Consider This

Social media posts are not always credible, or able to be trusted or believed. It's important to check the website that the post links to, and the author. What do you think are some other ways to tell if a post is trustworthy?

Words on a Page

Published documents can be primary sources. Publication is the printing of multiple copies of a document to be sold or distributed to people.

Newspapers and magazines are published documents. Articles in newspapers and magazines can be primary or secondary sources. If the author writes about seeing an event or gives an opinion about an event, the article is probably a primary source.

This **memorial**, called the White Rose Memorial in Munich, Bavaria, Germany, shows pamphlets that were written by students to oppose Nazis.

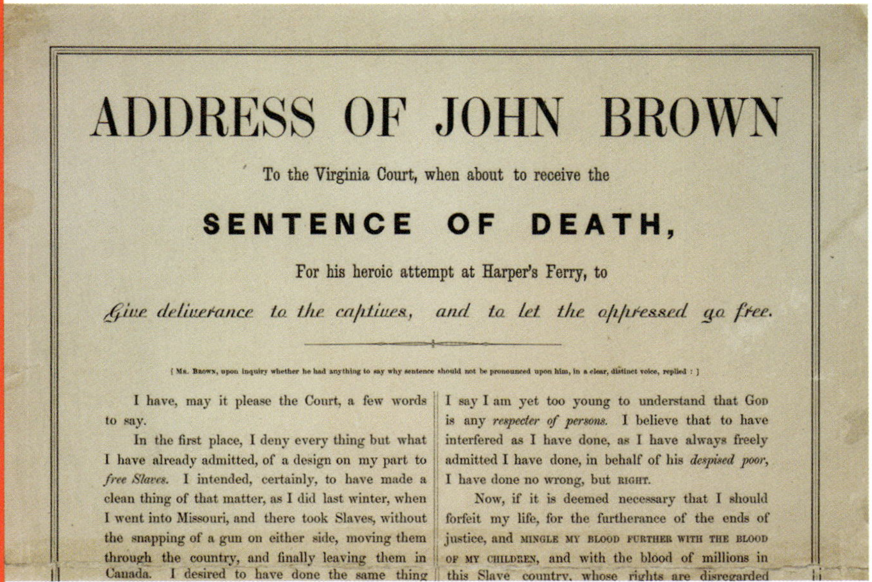

ADDRESS OF JOHN BROWN

To the Virginia Court, when about to receive the

SENTENCE OF DEATH,

For his heroic attempt at Harper's Ferry, to

Give deliverance to the captives, and to let the oppressed go free.

[Mr. Brown, upon inquiry whether he had anything to say why sentence should not be pronounced upon him, in a clear, distinct voice, replied :]

I have, may it please the Court, a few words to say.

In the first place, I deny every thing but what I have already admitted, of a design on my part to *free Slaves.* I intended, certainly, to have made a clean thing of that matter, as I did last winter, when I went into Missouri, and there took Slaves, without the snapping of a gun on either side, moving them through the country, and finally leaving them in Canada. I desired to have done the same thing

I say I am yet too young to understand that God is any *respecter of persons.* I believe that to have interfered as I have done, as I have always freely admitted I have done, in behalf of his *despised poor*, I have done no wrong, but RIGHT.

Now, if it is deemed necessary that I should forfeit my life, for the furtherance of the ends of justice, and MINGLE MY BLOOD FURTHER WITH THE BLOOD OF MY CHILDREN, and with the blood of millions in this Slave country, whose rights are disregarded

This broadside is a primary source that tells what abolitionist John Brown said to the court when he was about to be sentenced to death in 1859. An abolitionist is someone who fights slavery.

Broadsides and pamphlets are primary sources that were commonly published in the past. A broadside is a single large sheet of paper with printing on one side. In the days before TV, radio, and the internet, broadsides were among the quickest ways to spread information. For example, during the American Revolution, colonists passed around broadsides of the Declaration of Independence. Pamphlets are brief booklets that promote a specific view or provide information. They usually have between five and 48 pages, not including the cover page, and were popular until the early 20th century.

WORD WISE

A MEMORIAL IS A PLACE, DISPLAY, OR EVENT THAT SERVES AS A WAY TO REMEMBER SOMEONE OR SOMETHING THAT HAPPENED.

People Share Their Stories

Studying the written or spoken words of people who lived in the past can help us learn about their feelings regarding the events they experienced. Several types of primary sources tell people's own stories.

Autobiographies and memoirs are books about the author. A memoir usually focuses, or centers, on certain events in the author's life. An autobiography often concentrates on the author's entire life.

Prince Harry, a member of the British royal family, wrote a memoir about major life events titled *Spare*. It was published in 2023.

A member of the Evergreen Protective Association is working on an oral history interview. The Evergreen Protective Association was started in 1951 to work towards good connections between Black and white neighbors in Baltimore's Evergreen neighborhood.

Interviews let you know what people—some famous, some not—thought about the times they lived in. Oral history projects are collections of interviews, usually of people who lived through similar experiences. The Federal Writers' Project of the 1930s collected stories of former slaves. A more recent example is the South Asian Oral History project. It began in 2005 and records the experiences of South Asian **immigrants** in the Pacific Northwest.

WORD WISE

IMMIGRANTS ARE PEOPLE WHO COME TO A COUNTRY AND SETTLE THERE.

Secretive Sources

Many primary sources were never meant to be public. Letters were written for the people to whom they were sent. Journals and diaries are personal accounts, made for the writer's own use.

In past centuries, people in public life often kept diaries. These writings have become valuable sources for historians. The private, candid views written in personal journals help to show the full picture of an age. These primary sources can give details not found in official records or books, which may have been censored during that time.

Manuscripts are another type of unpublished primary source. One kind of manuscript is the text of a book before it is published. Looking at book manuscripts shows how an author's ideas changed in the course of writing. Books that were written before the invention of printing are also called manuscripts. Many of the earliest manuscripts were written on a material called papyrus. This material is made from plants which grow along the Nile River in Egypt.

This manuscript of *The Story of Ahiqar* was written on papyrus around the fifth century BCE.

compareandcontrast

In what ways do you think diaries and manuscripts are similar and different?

Diary entries by Nelson Mandela, South Africa's first Black president, can be found in the book *Letters to Myself*.

Government Accounts

It's important that governments keep records of what they do. These official records include laws, court cases, treaties, constitutions, and censuses. A constitution is a set of rules that guides how a country, state, or other political organization works. A census is a count of the people who live in a country. Some censuses also tell things about those people, such as their backgrounds, what they own, and how they live.

In ancient times, especially in the Middle East and China, governments kept lists of kings and wars. They also recorded events such as the building of temples and natural disasters. All these records are important primary sources.

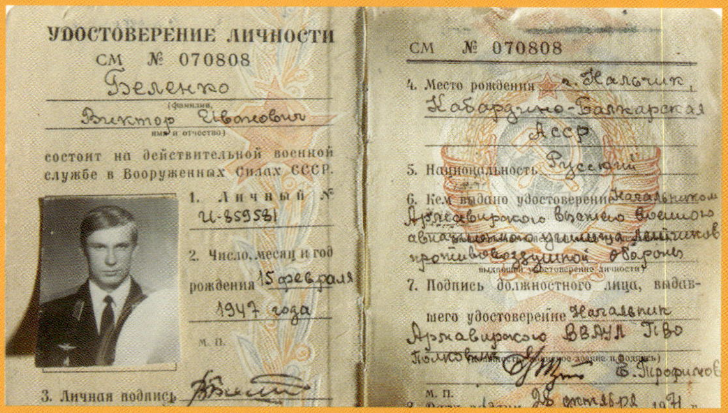

This military identification document for Soviet Union pilot Viktor Belenko is an official document and primary source found at the CIA Museum.

Inside this display tent at Salisbury Cathedral in Wiltshire, England, is a historical document called the Magna Carta. This document helped to **inspire** American colonists to fight during the American Revolution to defend certain rights the Magna Carta says should be given to all Englishmen.

Sometimes official records are discovered by chance. When Germany was defeated in World War II, the Nazis left behind many documents. Other times, documents are declassified by laws. For example, the Nazi War Crimes Disclosure Act allowed 400,000 pages of previously classified documents about Nazi **intelligence** gathered during World War II to become publicly available.

WORD WISE

TO INSPIRE IS TO CAUSE SOMEONE TO WANT TO DO SOMETHING. INTELLIGENCE IS A COLLECTION OF INFORMATION THAT IS VALUABLE POLITICALLY OR MILITARILY.

Beyond Written Words

Not all primary sources are written documents—many are images. These sources include drawings, sketches, photographs, cartoons, and maps. They give information, or facts, about people, places, objects, and events that words may not be able to describe.

Newspapers and magazines have printed drawings and photos, or pictures, of people and events since the 1800s. Advertisers and businesses use photography to show people their products.

This political cartoon from 1913 aims to show how banks and politics can be connected. It shows how banks can control politics and how politics can control banks.

A woman holds a powder horn map. These maps were considered the first road maps of America. They included **engravings** that showed early American cities, such as New York and Quebec, and the trails that led to them.

Cartoons are drawings that make a point, tell a joke, or tell a story. Political cartoons **criticize** the government or make fun of it. These cartoons are usually single drawings, but there are some political comic strips.

Maps can also be primary sources, and there are different kinds. Topographic maps show the location and shape of natural features such as mountains. The boundaries of countries, states, provinces, and cities are shown on political maps.

WORD WISE

TO CRITICIZE IS TO TALK ABOUT THE PROBLEMS OR FAULTS OF SOMEONE OR SOMETHING, OR TO EXPRESS DISAPPROVAL OF SOMEONE OR SOMETHING. AN ENGRAVING IS AN OBJECT ONTO WHICH AN ARTIST CUTS A DESIGN.

Video and Sound

Primary sources can also be recordings of audio, or sound, and video. Examples include movies, TV and radio shows, news broadcasts, and music.

Some of the oldest video primary sources are newsreels. Theaters in the early 1900s showed these short films about current events. Early audio primary sources include recordings of ordinary Americans playing folk and blues music, made in the 1930s.

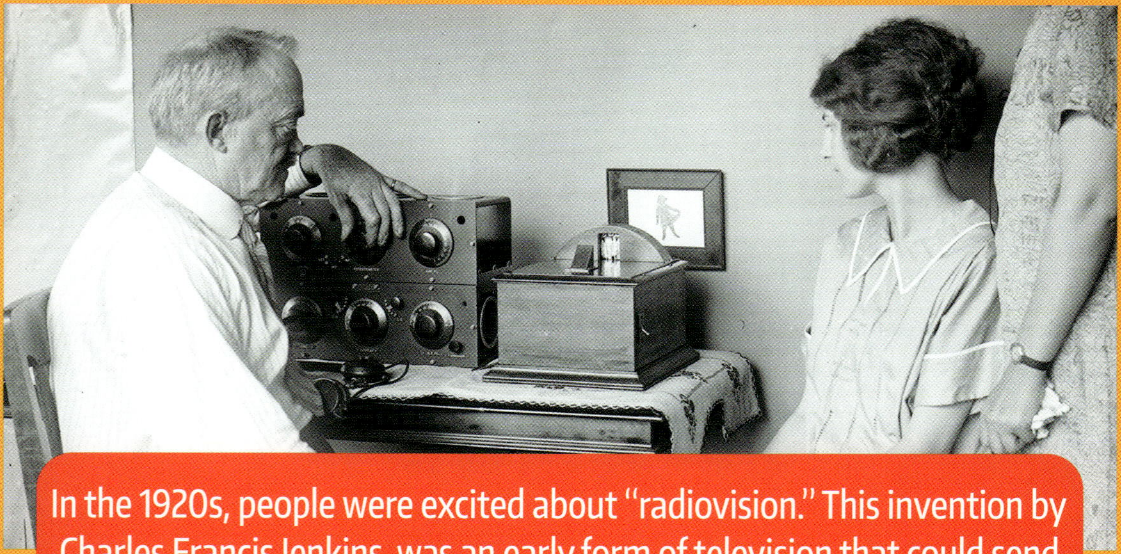

In the 1920s, people were excited about "radiovision." This invention by Charles Francis Jenkins was an early form of television that could send shadow-like images to other locations.

Over the last 10 years, the number of Americans who listen to podcasts and other forms of online audio has steadily increased.

Since those times, many important speeches have been recorded. Between 1933 and 1944, U.S. president Franklin D. Roosevelt delivered a series of radio addresses, called fireside chats, to explain his policies to the American people.

The first radio station started broadcasting in Pittsburgh, Pennsylvania, in 1920. Within two years, hundreds of radio stations opened. Radio was a major source of information and entertainment until the mid-1950s. Then television, or TV, became more popular. Many people still watch TV today, but they also get information from online videos, articles, and podcasts.

Consider This

What do you think people in years to come could learn about the audio and video primary sources popular today, such as podcasts and online videos?

Tools, Tombs, Trash—and More!

Documents, images, and recordings can provide many facts and clues about the past. However, some cultures did not leave these kinds of primary sources behind. Not all cultures use writing. If you want to study these cultures, you need to look at other kinds of records, such as artifacts.

Artifacts are objects made by humans. They can tell us things about the time when they were made.

Ancient tombs can be found on what's called the Royal Wall in the ancient city of Nabataean in today's Petra, Jordan. Tombs are a home or house for those who have died.

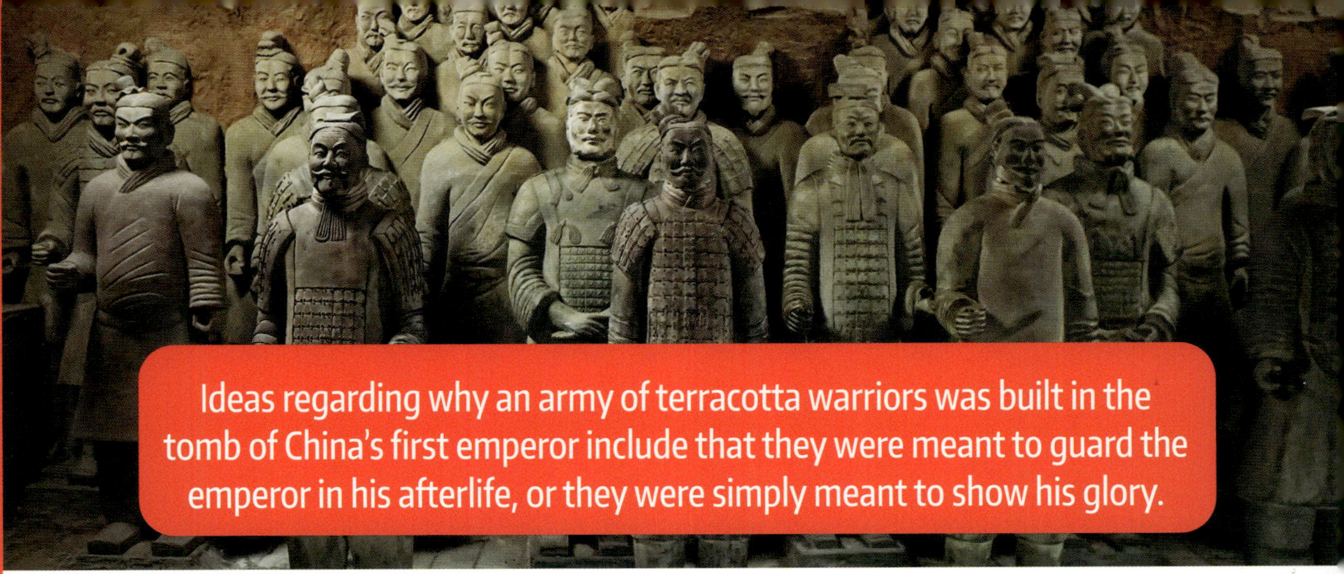

Ideas regarding why an army of terracotta warriors was built in the tomb of China's first emperor include that they were meant to guard the emperor in his afterlife, or they were simply meant to show his glory.

The earliest stone tools are artifacts. So are the household objects thrown in the trash today. Everything made by human beings—from simple tools to complex machines, from the earliest houses and tombs to modern skyscrapers—is an artifact.

Sometimes people in the present aren't sure how people in the past used a particular artifact. For example, an army of more than 8,000 soldiers made from terracotta was found in the tomb of China's first emperor, Qin Shi Huang, and nobody is quite sure why the army was built!

Consider This

Terracotta is a type of ceramic pottery. It starts as clay and it hardens when it is heated at high temperatures. What would you make if given some terracotta clay? It might become an artifact!

Putting Primary Sources to Use

Learning about history through primary sources can help with understanding historical events and how people experienced these events. Reading the words written by people in the past, hearing their voices, or seeing what they looked like can bring the past to life. Primary sources make it easier to understand that people in history had beliefs, hopes, and dreams, just like people do today.

Historians use primary sources to write about past events. When they do, they make interpretations. They choose which events or which people to focus on. They give their own ideas about the causes or consequences of events.

When you look at primary sources yourself, you become the historian. Since primary sources only offer a snapshot of history, they can be a starting point for questions and the gathering of further evidence that can provide a rich understanding of history.

Secondary sources, such as books written by historians, can be used along with primary sources to understand history.

compareandcontrast

How are primary and secondary sources similar and different? Why do you think both might be important when studying people or events in history?

This photo taken in 2022 could be considered a primary source that shows how fishing is a main form of livelihood in Anakao, Madagascar.

The Creator's Point of View

When studying a primary source, it's important to keep in mind the point of view of who created it. For every primary source you look at, think about who created it and how that person relates to the information provided. For example, a person's knowledge depends on their education and experience. Also consider how a person's background—their age, job, social class, race, religion, nationality, and so on—might affect how they see a situation.

This image shows propaganda that was created to interest German youth in following Hitler and his Nazi party. The Nazi party used propaganda to gain support among Germans for actions that were later deemed crimes against humanity.

The internet can spread propaganda, misinformation, and disinformation. Misinformation is information that by definition is incorrect, but it could be false by accident. Disinformation is wrong and meant to deceive, or mislead, others.

Some primary sources make no attempt to be unbiased. Opinion pieces, such as editorials, are meant to convince others that something is true. Political speeches try to persuade people to vote for a candidate.

Propaganda is information used to influence public opinion or even to change people's beliefs. It can be facts, half-truths, and even lies. Propaganda is spread through mass media, which includes TV, print ads, artwork, and other forms of expression that reach a large audience.

Consider This

Unbiased means that someone or something isn't biased, or shows an unfair tendency to believe certain ideas or people are better than others . What are some ways you can tell if a primary source is unbiased?

Difficulties of Using Primary Sources

Although they are important, it's not always easy to work with primary sources. Many are written in languages other than English. Some have been translated into English, but many have not. Some are written in languages that are no longer spoken. A few are written in languages that no one alive knows how to translate. Even sources in English may be hard to understand because of the more formal way that people used to write. Handwriting styles from the past can be challenging to read too.

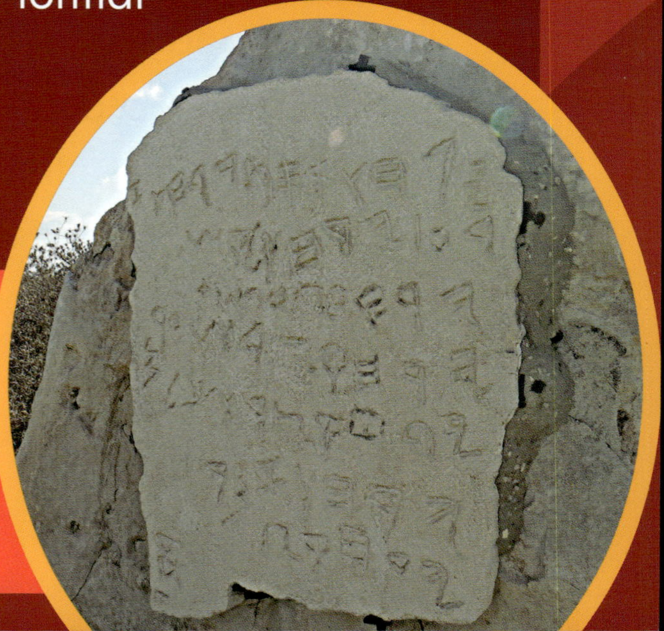

The Gezer Calendar shown here provides information about life in ancient Israel. However, it is written in Hebrew and would be difficult, or hard, to understand without knowing this language!

This artifact is one of many that were destroyed by the Islamic State when it occupied the ancient city of Palmyra twice between 2015 and 2017.

Finding primary sources can be difficult as well. Countless documents and works of art have been destroyed, or ruined, over the years—some in fires or wars, some eaten by pests, and others because they became fragile, or easily broken, and eventually turned to dust. It can also be hard to find primary sources that truly reflect life for **minority** groups. Many primary sources can show negative attitudes about certain minority groups that were popular during a time period, but that today are considered unacceptable.

WORD WISE

A MINORITY IS A GROUP OF PEOPLE WHO SHARE A CERTAIN CULTURE, LANGUAGE, OR RELIGION AND WHOSE POPULATION IS LESS THAN HALF OF THE POPULATION OF AN ENTIRE COUNTRY OR OTHER REGION.

Places to Discover Primary Sources

There are many ways to keep primary sources safe. When possible, they are kept in their original form. Sometimes paper copies are made. Digital copies may be stored on computers. Important records are often collected in archives, museums, and libraries.

Records from ancient time periods may have been written on stone. These primary sources may be buried in the ground or partially destroyed. Historians work to uncover these records. For example, historians know about the laws made by the Babylonian king Hammurabi because the laws were inscribed on a stone pillar. The pillar, made in the 1700s BCE, was discovered in 1901.

Historians also use the tools of archaeology to study ancient times. Archaeology is the study of things, such as tools and structures, that people created and used in the past, then left behind.

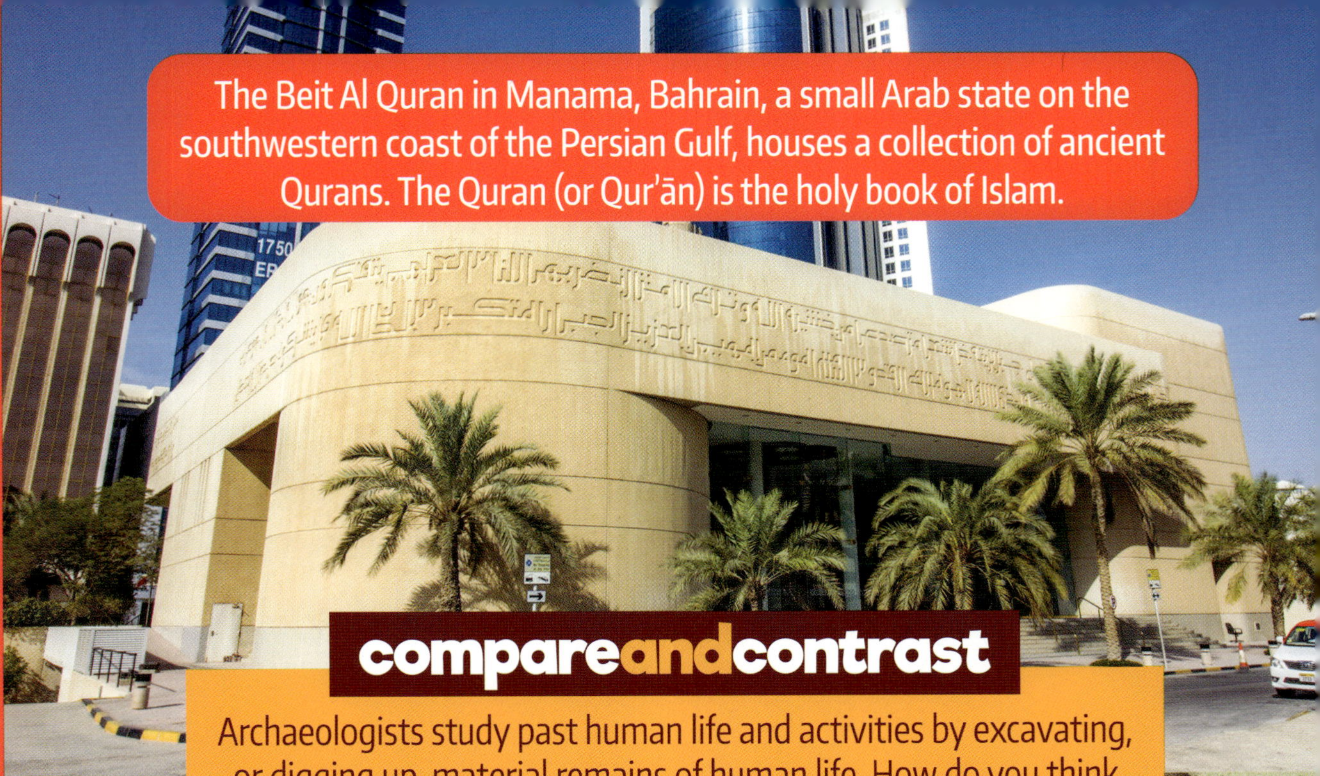

The Beit Al Quran in Manama, Bahrain, a small Arab state on the southwestern coast of the Persian Gulf, houses a collection of ancient Qurans. The Quran (or Qur'ān) is the holy book of Islam.

compare and contrast

Archaeologists study past human life and activities by excavating, or digging up, material remains of human life. How do you think archaeologists and historians are similar and different?

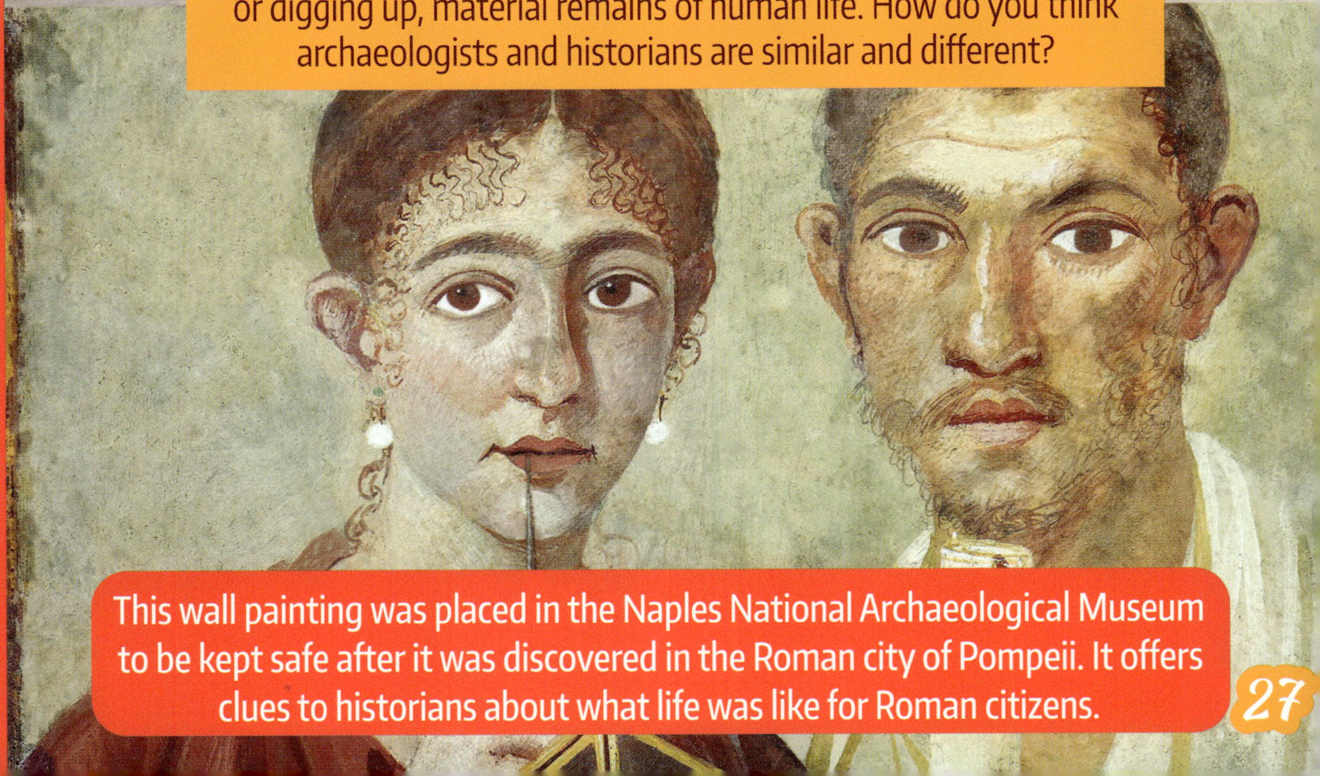

This wall painting was placed in the Naples National Archaeological Museum to be kept safe after it was discovered in the Roman city of Pompeii. It offers clues to historians about what life was like for Roman citizens.

Understanding the Past, Present, and Future

Studying history allows people to have the skills and tools to understand problems people faced in the past. They can then identify patterns of problems that may have continued into the present, and then address these problems. In this way, studying history and primary sources helps people to understand the things that are happening today and to guess what may happen in the future, or time to come.

Artifacts and primary sources can help people understand how they have similar and different experiences than those who lived in the past. For example, this pottery from ancient Greece shows the timeless connection between a mother and a child.

This photo could be considered a primary source related to the Flint water **crisis**.

For example, understanding the history of public health can help explain why people with less money faced more problems when the water supply of Flint, Michigan, was found to have unsafe levels of lead from April 2014 to June 2016. Primary sources can be key to understanding the effects historical events such as this had on people, and the importance of preventing their recurrence in the future.

WORD WISE

A CRISIS IS AN UNSTABLE OR DIFFICULT SITUATION.

Glossary

archive A place in which public records or historical documents are preserved.

broadcast A single radio or television program.

candid Frank, open, and honest.

censor To closely review books, movies, letters, and other media to remove language that could be considered harmful to society, immoral, or offensive.

complex Challenging to explain or understand.

consequence The result or effect of something.

culture The beliefs and ways of life of a group of people.

declassify To allow the public to view or learn about something that had been classified, or secret.

dictionary An alphabetically arranged list of words and their definitions.

document A formal piece of writing.

encyclopedia A set of articles, published in books or on the internet, that provides general information about different topics.

evidence Something that helps show or disprove the truth of something.

inscribe To write, engrave, or print something on a surface.

interpret To explain the meaning of something.

translate To change from one language or set of symbols into another.

For More Information

Books

Spanier, Kristine. *Using Primary Sources.* Minneapolis, MN: Pogo/Jump!, Inc., 2019.

Tait, Leia. *Primary Sources.* New York, NY: Weigl, 2020.

Websites

How Do You Know If a Source Is Valid?
wonderopolis.org/wonder/How-Do-You-Know-if-a-Source-is-Valid
Learn about how you can determine if a source is trustworthy here.

Primary Source
kids.britannica.com/kids/article/primary-source/629043
Learn more about primary sources and find more examples here.

Publisher's note to educators and parents: Our editors have carefully reviewed these websites to ensure that they are suitable for students. Many websites change frequently, however, and we cannot guarantee that a site's future contents will continue to meet our high standards of quality and educational value. Be advised that students should be closely supervised whenever they access the internet.

Index